REALLY STRANGE
REPTILES

THERESE SHEA

PowerKiDS
press

New York

Published in 2017 by The Rosen Publishing Group, Inc.
29 East 21st Street, New York, NY 10010

First Edition

Editor: Theresa Morlock
Book Design: Reann Nye

Photo Credits: Cover, p. 1 (reptile) DEA/DANI-JESKE/De Agostini Picture Library/Getty Images; cover, pp. 1–32 (background) Toa55/Shutterstock.com; p. 5 (chameleon) Fedor Selivanov/Shutterstock.com; p. 5 (turtle) Steve Byland/Shutterstock.com; p. 5 (lizard) forest71/Shutterstock.colm; p. 5 (snake) nawawi/Shutterstock.com; p. 5 (crocodile) Steven_Mol/Shutterstock.com; p. 6 Dennis W Donohue/ Shutterstock.com; p. 7 Jason Mintzer/Shutterstock.com; p. 8 Joe McDonald/Shutterstock.com; p. 9 John Cancalosi/Photolibrary/Getty Images; p. 10 Robin Eicher/EyeEm/Getty Images; pp. 11, 26 Michael & Patricia Fogden/Minden Pictures/Getty Images; p. 12 David C Azor/ Shutterstock.com; p. 13 Matt Cornish/Shutterstock.com; p. 14 Sista Vongjintanarug/Shutterstock.com; p. 15 Sergio Gutierrez Getino/Shutterstock.com; pp. 16, 17 (speckled padloper tortoise) Joel Sartore/ National Geographic/Getty Images; p. 17 (Galapagos tortoise) Keith Levit/Getty Images; p. 18 Picture by Tambako the Jaguar/Moment/Getty Images; p. 19 TOM MCHUGH/Science Source/ Getty Images; p. 21 (panther chameleon) Danita Delimont/Gallo Images/Getty Images; p. 21 (Jackson's chameleon, strange-nosed chameleon) reptiles4all/Shutterstock.com; p. 22 Auscape/ Universal Images Group Editorial/Getty Images; p. 23 Stephen Dalton/Minden Pictures/Getty Images; p. 25 Nature/UIG/Universal Images Group/Getty Images; p. 27 Roger de Montfort/Shutterstock.com; p. 29 Dennis van de Water/Shutterstock.com; p. 30 (scales) saiko3p/Shutterstock.com; p. 30 (breathe air) Rick Sause Photography/Shutterstock.com; p. 30 (reptile eggs) WeStudio/Shutterstock.com; p. 30 (insect eating) chockdee Romkaew/Shutterstock.com.

Library of Congress Cataloging-in-Publication Data

Cataloging-in-Publication Data
Names: Shea, Therese.
Title: Really strange reptiles! / Therese Shea.
Description: New York : Gareth Stevens Publishing, 2017. | Series: Really strange adaptations| Includes index.
Identifiers: ISBN 9781499427929 (pbk.) | ISBN 9781499428469 (library bound) | ISBN 9781508153023 (6 pack)
Subjects: LCSH: Reptiles-Juvenile literature.
Classification: LCC QL644.2 S54 2017 | DDC 597.9–dc23

Manufactured in the United States of America

CPSIA Compliance Information: Batch #BW17PK: For Further Information contact Rosen Publishing, New York, New York at 1-800-237-9932

CONTENTS

AMAZING AND ODD ADAPTATIONS

What would happen if a shark had no fins? What if a squirrel was pink? What if a robin didn't lay its eggs in a nest? These animals probably couldn't survive. The shark wouldn't be able to swim. Predators would easily spot the squirrel. Without a nest, the robin's eggs would become tasty snacks for other animals.

Adaptations are the traits, or features, of an animal that make it better suited to its **habitat**. These may include what the animal looks like, how it acts, or how the inside of its body works.

Modern reptiles have **developed** adaptations that have helped them outlast other animals. They've been around for more than 300 million years. Some reptile adaptations may seem weird—but they work!

These are some well-known reptiles. Have you ever wondered why they look and act like they do? These are adaptations!

THE TRICKY HORNED TOAD

You might wonder why an animal called a horned toad is in a book about reptiles—it's actually a lizard! That's not the only thing that's weird about this creature. It has horns on its head and spikes on its back. The lizard's coloring—yellow, gray, or reddish-brown—matches its desert and **semi-arid** habitats in North and Central America, but it can change its color to look a bit darker or lighter.

The horned toad's body is low to the ground like a toad's. Its nose is a bit like a toad's, too. That's how this lizard got its name.

ECTOTHERMIC ANIMALS

People and other mammals are warm-blooded. That means their inner body temperature remains the same no matter their surroundings. Reptiles—including the horned toad—are cold-blooded, or ectothermic. That means they must use their actions and **environment** to keep their body working at the best temperature. They warm up in the hot sun and cool down in the shade. Body temperature is important in keeping the body's organs working correctly. Cold reptiles often lack energy.

The horned toad's color and shape help it blend in and look like rocks. This is a good trick to surprise its prey—mostly ants—but also to escape predators. Horned toads have quite a few predators, such as hawks, roadrunners, snakes, cats, dogs, wolves, coyotes, and other lizards. Luckily, horned toads have a few more tricks, too.

When cornered by a predator, a horned toad can puff itself up to twice its original size by swallowing air. It looks a bit like a balloon with spines. Sometimes, this scares a predator—or at least makes it think it might not want to swallow something that's so pointy.

Horned toads don't have to use their blood-squirting defense very often.

If that doesn't work, the lizard uses one of the strangest defenses in the animal kingdom: it shoots blood out of its eyes! The blood comes out of the corners of its eyes and usually only travels a few feet. The horned toad seems to aim at a predator's face. This defense may be meant to shock or confuse predators. However, chemicals in the blood also taste bad to dogs and wolves, making them think a horned toad wouldn't be a good dinner.

THE ABNORMAL GHARIAL

If you spot a gharial in the water, at first you might think it's a crocodile. Look again and you'll see the gharial's long, narrow **snout**. This species, or kind, of reptile lives in the rivers of northern India and Nepal. Its special snout allows it to whip its head quickly through the water to grab prey.

crocodile

LOOK UP!

Gharials, crocodiles, and alligators are all reptiles called crocodilians. All are cold-blooded so they must warm up in the sun when they can. Recently, scientists have been studying alligators and crocodiles that climb trees to find a warm, sunny spot. The creatures may climb trees to keep an eye out for prey as well. Adult crocodiles have been spotted as high up as 6 feet (1.8 m), while young crocodiles climb even higher.

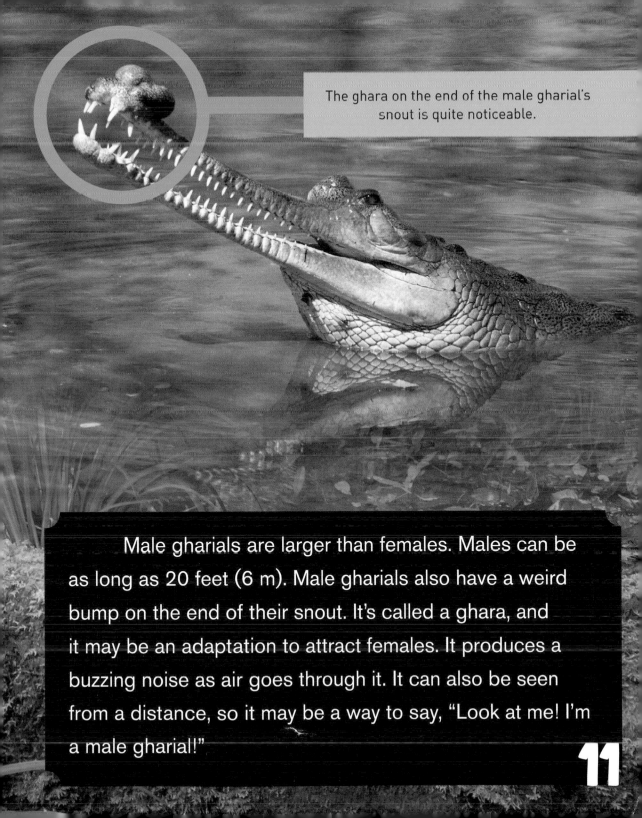

The ghara on the end of the male gharial's snout is quite noticeable.

Male gharials are larger than females. Males can be as long as 20 feet (6 m). Male gharials also have a weird bump on the end of their snout. It's called a ghara, and it may be an adaptation to attract females. It produces a buzzing noise as air goes through it. It can also be seen from a distance, so it may be a way to say, "Look at me! I'm a male gharial!"

THE PECULIAR
BEARDED DRAGON

Bearded dragons don't actually have beards. However, the fold of loose skin hanging from their neck, called a dewlap, looks a bit like a beard. It's not just skin—it has spiky scales, too. Bearded dragons can make it puff out. They do this to scare away other bearded dragons or to attract mates. They can turn the beard gray or black.

Both male and female bearded dragons have beards. Bearded dragons are only found in Australia, where they live in many kinds of habitats.

Waving is another strange behavior of the bearded dragon. They stand on three legs and move one leg in a circle. Scientists think they do this to show that they don't want to fight with a larger, tougher bearded dragon. Bearded dragons also bob their head toward a possible **mate** or a weaker reptile.

THE FRILLED DRAGON

The frilled dragon (or frilled lizard) has a special kind of skin flap around its neck. This Australian reptile has predators such as other lizards, birds of prey, and snakes. When the frilled dragon feels threatened, it rises on its back legs, opens its mouth, spreads its colorful flap, and hisses. If that doesn't scare the predator away, the frilled dragon flees and runs up a tree.

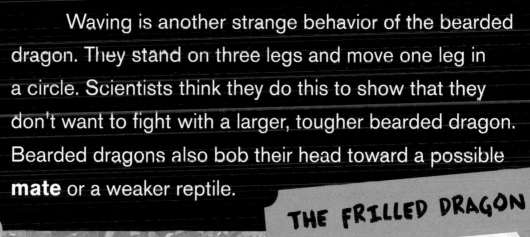

TOTALLY WEIRD TURTLES

The alligator snapping turtle is a freshwater turtle found in the United States. It can grow to be longer than 28 inches (71 cm) and weigh as much as 155 pounds (70 kg). It's sometimes called the dinosaur of the turtle world because of its large claws and hooked jaws, as well as the ridges on its shell.

The alligator snapping turtle is omnivorous. That means it eats both animals and plants.

If you've ever been fishing, you'll understand why the alligator snapping turtle has its weird tongue. Its tongue has a worm-shaped bit that sticks out on the end. It turns pink when the turtle is looking for food. The snapping turtle opens its mouth, lets its tongue wiggle in the water, and waits for prey. When a fish spots the "worm," it swims right into the turtle's mouth and—SNAP!

SUCH A STINKER

The skunk has a famous defense—a stinky spray that it **emits** when it's in danger. You might be surprised to know that some reptiles also produce a gross-smelling odor. The well-named stinkpot turtle, or musk turtle, can release an awful-smelling liquid when it's scared. This makes some predators leave it alone.

Turtles have a great defense—their shell. They can pull their head into the shell and protect themselves from predators who can't bite through it. The big-headed turtle of Asia is different: its head is too big to pull into its shell. Instead, it has other adaptations to keep its head safe. The big-headed turtle has a skull of solid bone as well as a kind of bony armor on the top and sides of its head. A big head has its advantages, too. This turtle has large jaws that are so powerful it can bite through the hard outer covering of shellfish.

The big-headed turtle is also known for its tail, which can be as long as the rest of its body. It uses the tail for balance when climbing.

The big-headed turtle is now **endangered**. People hunt it for food in its habitat in China.

Galápagos tortoise

CHELONIANS

What's the difference between a turtle and a tortoise? Turtles live most of their lives in water, while tortoises live on land. Reptiles called terrapins live partly in water—often salty water—and partly on land near water. All three kinds of reptiles are called chelonians. They can range in size from the speckled padloper tortoise, which is just 1.5 inches (3.8 cm) long, to the Galápagos tortoise, which can be 5 feet (1.52 m) long.

speckled padloper tortoise

THE FREAKY FLYING GECKO

Geckos are small lizards that are excellent climbers. There are about 1,000 species and all live in warm parts of the world. Geckos are so good at climbing because many kinds have special pads on their toes. The pads have tiny hooks that grab onto surfaces—geckos can even walk across ceilings!

The flying gecko also has skin that is perfect **camouflage** for its life among trees.

There are several species of flying geckos. They can't really fly, but they do have an adaptation for their forest homes. They stretch out their legs and tail to create a large, flat shape. Then, they glide on the air from tree to tree, sometimes as far as 200 feet (61 m). This is a great way to escape from predators such as snakes.

19

THE CREEPY CHAMELEON

The chameleon's ability to change color is well known, but that doesn't make it any less odd—or amazing! There are about 150 species of these lizards.

The chameleon's skin doesn't change. Instead, the cells of its skin contain pigment, which is a matter that gives things colors. To change the color of its skin, the reptile changes the placement of its cells, bringing them closer together or moving them farther apart. Its color appears to change as it does this.

People once thought chameleons changed color to match their surroundings. However, scientists have learned this isn't true. Males turn colors to attract mates and scare away other males. They also change colors depending on light, temperature, and even emotions such as fear.

THE SKIN THEY'RE IN

Have you ever wondered why reptiles have such thick, scaly skin? It keeps moisture, or wetness, in their bodies. That makes sure the reptiles that live in dry, hot deserts don't lose too much water through their skin. The scales that cover reptile bodies are made of keratin, which is the same matter our nails are made of. Keratin is made of many layers of thin, flat cells. Spikes and horns on lizards are made of harder keratin.

Jackson's chameleon

Male chameleons turn the brightest colors.

panther chameleon

strange-nosed chameleon

Changing colors isn't the only thing that makes chameleons stand out in the animal world. Chameleons have special eyes. Each of its two eyes can move separately in a different direction, at the same time if needed. This means that chameleons have a wide range of vision. They can look two ways at once.

Chameleons have a cone-shaped eyelid surrounding each eye.

When chameleon eyes work together, they can make faraway objects look larger and clearer, somewhat like looking through the lens of a camera. This helps them find prey, such as insects and even birds. A chameleon's sticky tongue can be twice the length of its body. It shoots out its tongue to capture its meal, and then reels it back into its mouth.

THE MYSTERIOUS MEXICAN MOLE LIZARD

If the chameleon's coloring wows you, the Mexican mole lizard's coloring may too. This odd-looking reptile doesn't need skin pigment called melanin to protect it from the sun's rays. It doesn't need coloring to camouflage itself because it mostly lives underground.

The Mexican mole lizard only has front legs. It pushes itself through tunnels in the ground. The reptiles don't even use their front legs much, except to push dirt and sand out of the way. Scientists can see with **X-rays** that the Mexican mole lizard once had back legs, too. There are leftover bones in its body that show this. However, those back legs disappeared at some point in time, perhaps because it was easier for the animals to move without them.

24

A Mexican mole lizard is a kind of reptile called an amphisbaenian. The other reptiles in this group don't have any limbs at all.

SERIOUSLY STRANGE SNAKES

Snakes have plenty of weird adaptations, too. A sidewinder travels by moving sideways. Why can't it just slither in a straight line? This form of locomotion, or movement, is an adaptation.

I'LL HAVE THE SNAILS!

One kind of snake has adapted to eat snails. Snails are soft-bodied creatures with hard shells to protect them from predators. However, snail-eating snakes have jaws made just for eating them! Their upper jaw holds on to the shell, while the lower jaw and teeth can move to pull the body of the snail from the shell. Most snails have shells that twist in a **clockwise** direction, which is why these snakes have more teeth on the right side.

Sidewinders make special tracks as they move. Their body blends in with the desert sand!

There are four species of sidewinders, also called horn vipers. They live in the deserts of North America, Africa, and the Middle East. They move in such an odd way so that only two parts of their body are touching the superhot sand at a time. This is so the sidewinder's body won't get too hot, which is a danger for reptiles and other cold-blooded animals in the desert. Sidewinders also sometimes bury part of their body for the same reason.

The Malagasy leaf-nosed snake is named for its strange snout. With its shape and coloring, it easily blends in with the trees and bushes in which it lives. Malagasy leaf-nosed snakes **ambush** frogs, small reptiles, and sometimes birds. However, scientists aren't really sure why they have their special nose.

Baby Malagasy leaf-nosed snakes have an odd behavior. They hang straight down from branches. They may be trying to look like the seeds of some plants in their Madagascar habitat, but no one knows why this is helpful to them.

As you can see, there's still plenty to learn about reptile adaptations. Maybe someday you'll study some truly odd adaptations and solve these mysteries.

Malagasy leaf-nosed snakes have a bite that's painful, but not deadly to humans.

COMMON REPTILE ADAPTATIONS

ADAPTATION
most lay hard-shelled or leathery-shelled eggs

WHY
young in eggs with thick shells can survive better on dry land

ADAPTATION
breathe air through lungs

WHY
allows reptile to travel away from watery habitats

ADAPTATION
scales on skin

WHY
keep reptile body from drying out, especially in hot places

ADAPTATION
ectothermic (cold-blooded)

WHY
allows reptile to need less food for energy to keep body warm

You've learned about many odd reptile adaptations, but the adaptations that many of them have in common are just as amazing!

GLOSSARY

ambush: To attack by surprise from a hidden place.

camouflage: Colors or shapes on animals that allow them to blend in with their surroundings.

clockwise: In the direction that the hands of a clock move.

develop: To grow or advance.

emit: To send out from a source.

endangered: In danger of dying out.

environment: The conditions that surround a living thing and affect the way it lives.

habitat: The natural home for plants, animals, and other living things.

mate: A partner for making babies, or to come together to make babies.

semi-arid: Having light yearly rainfall.

snout: An animal's nose and mouth.

X-rays: Powerful invisible rays that can pass through objects and make it possible to see inside things such as a body.

INDEX

WEBSITES

Due to the changing nature of Internet links, PowerKids Press has developed an online list of websites related to the subject of this book. This site is updated regularly. Please use this link to access the list: www.powerkidslinks.com/rsa/rep